Coloring Book

ANIMALS
of
AFRICA

Mark Shawe

Book Series: Animal Planet

In this Coloring Book you will find:

- 20 original realistic full-page images of wild animals of Africa on single-sided sheets to prevent bleed-through
- 60 interesting unusual facts about the animals

Grab you favorite tool: pencils, crayons, markers or paints, and start coloring!

ISBN: 9781079227536

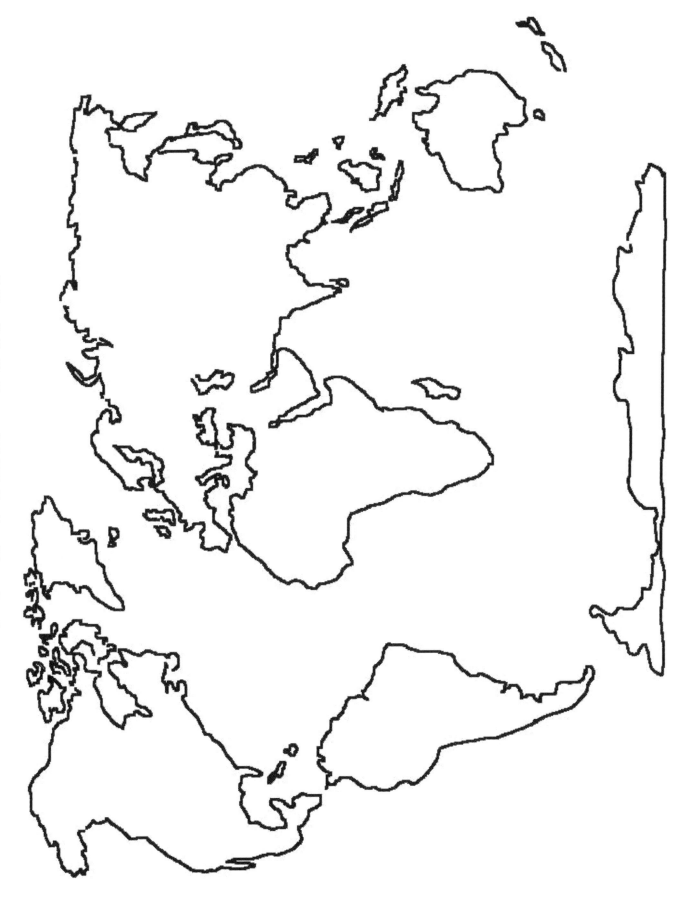

WORLD MAP

Black Buffalo

Here's a fine example of pure democracy – buffalos actually vote on where to move next as a herd! They stand up head first in the direction they want to go and then the dominant female leads the entire herd in the direction picked by the majority! Did someone teach them that?

life expectancy in nature

0   **20**   25   50   75   100

weigh up to   1000 kg (2200 lb)

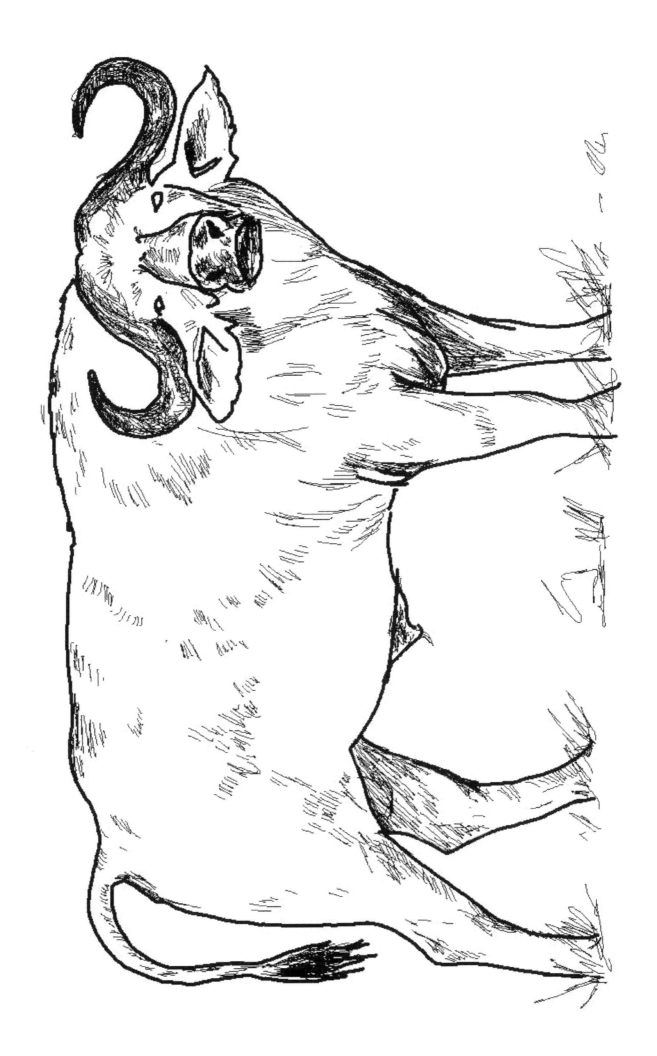

Antelope

Well, believe it or not, people have something in common with antelopes! The horns (just kidding!). It's not the horns themselves but the substance they are covered with. It's called keratin, and that's what our nails are made of! Cute! Remember, there are 91 kinds of them, so whatever colors you choose to color the picture with, you'd probably hit the bull's eye.

life expectancy in nature

0   **15**   25   50   75   100

weigh up to   280 kg (615 lb)

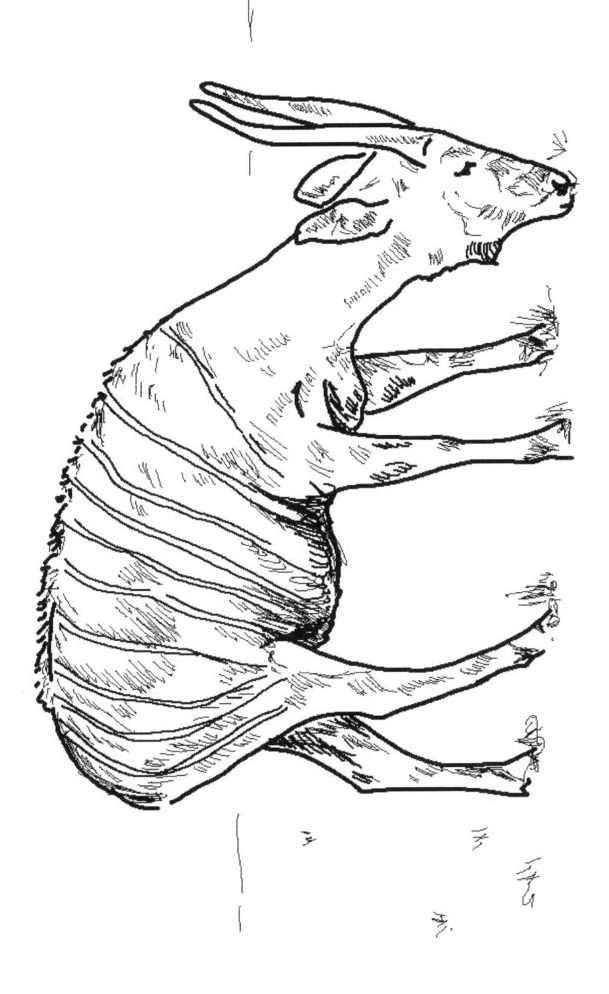

Bat-eared Fox

Well, if you want a pet that will protect you from scorpions and millipedes, make sure you take a bat-eared fox with you, since these cute animals feed on such creepy creatures. Most of their diet consists of termites, though.

life expectancy in nature

0   **13**   25   50   75   100

weigh up to   4.5 kg (9,9 lb)

Toucan

Toucan's beak looks heavy but in fact is it porous inside, so the weight is not what it seems. Just like woodpeckers, toucans make nests in the hollows of trees.

life expectancy in nature

50

0   25   50   75   100

weigh up to   0.7 kg (1,54 lb)

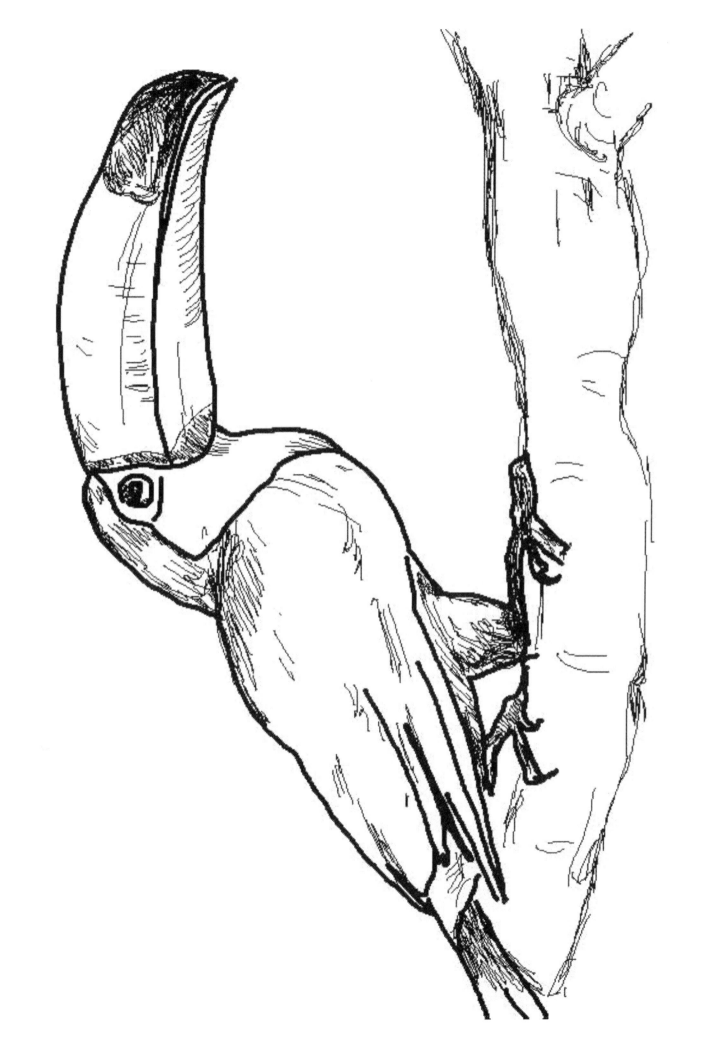

Lion

Have you every seen a lion wandering about his cage looking for prey? Right, never! That's because lions are the laziest big cats in the world! They don't bother moving during daylight even in the wild when it's too hot. Make sure to check out ligers, tigons, leopons or jaglions sometime. These are hybrids from breeding lions in captivity.

.

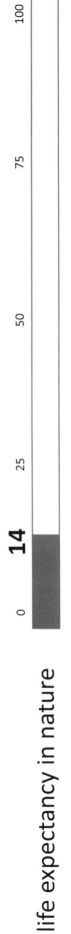

life expectancy in nature

0   **14**   25   50   75   100

weigh up to   250 kg (550 lb)

Elephants

Are you scared of bees? Don't worry! You are not alone! Elephants are afraid of them, too! These giants have lots of human-like emotions, they can feel very sad for a long time if they lose a member of the family, and even cry. Or they smile like kids and express tons of joy when they swim and splash in the water!

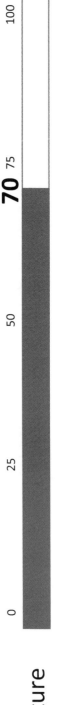

life expectancy in nature

| 0 | 25 | 50 | **70** | 75 | 100 |

weigh up to   5000 kg (11000 lb)

Aardvark

Apart from being the best diggers in the world, aardvarks have a very useful feature – they can close up their nostrils when they dig to keep dirt and dust from coming into their noses! Wish people could do that while diving!

life expectancy in nature

0   18   25   50   75   100

weigh up to   70 kg (155 lb)

Zebra

We could learn a lot from zebras. For example, when someone bullies someone else, we could form a circle around this poor soul and defend him on all sides! That's what zebras do – they never let one of their own have an unfair fight with an enemy!

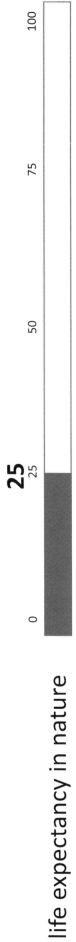

25

life expectancy in nature

weigh up to   350 kg (770 lb)

0   25   50   75   100

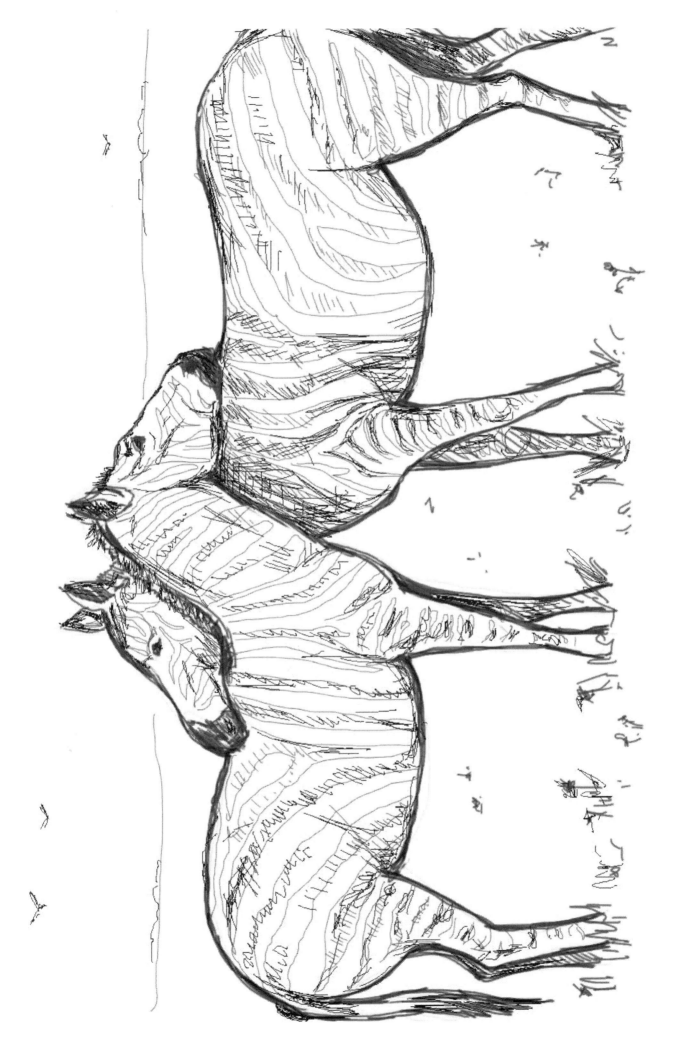

Gorilla

Ok, here comes the most hilarious fact about gorillas, we bet you've never heard of! Are you ready? Here we go - the word 'gorilla' comes from a Greek word meaning 'tribe of hairy women'!

life expectancy in nature

0   25   **48**50   75   100

weigh up to   250 kg (550 lb)

Gazelle

Gazelles have way too many enemies. But they were gifted with amazing eyesight, sense of hearing and smell. They can detect predators from afar. They can also do tricky jumps – with all four legs in the air! It's called 'pronking'. (Not to be tried by humans!)

life expectancy in nature

0   **7**   25   50   75   100

weigh up to   28 kg (62 lb)

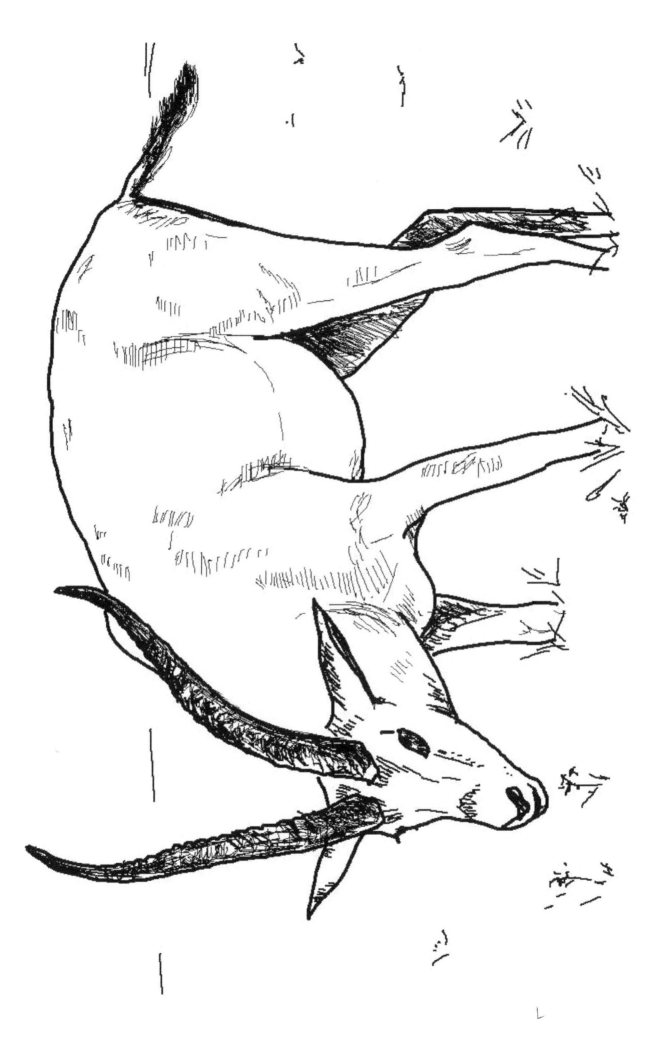

Rhino

These may look fierce, but the truth is rhinos aren't predators, they feed on vegetation. Not being very sociable among themselves they have but one friend – a bird! Birds, like the oxpeckers, ride on their backs and pull out insects and bugs which get into their skin and even warn rhinos when enemies approach!

life expectancy in nature

0   25   **35**   50   75   100

weigh up to   3000 kg (6600 lb)

Cheetah

Cheetah is a perfect running machine. Each body part is designed for speed, and fast speed at that! Going at 75 miles per hour they leave zero chance for the prey to survive. If you had a tail like cheetah's, you could make sharp turns as you run without ever slowing down!

life expectancy in nature

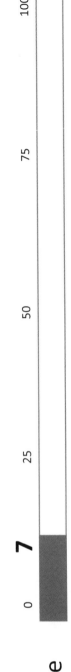

0   **7**   25   50   75   100

weigh up to   55 kg (120 lb)

Hippo

Hippos, or 'river horses', have a unique skin which needs to be kept wet all the time! Imagine soaking in a bathtub for 16 hours! However, they can't swim. They have the loudest voice in Africa – sort of like standing in front of speakers at a rock concert!

life expectancy in nature

0   25   50   **60**   75   100

weigh up to   4500 kg (9920 lb)

Baboon

Baboons have been given a very useful feature – a rough nerveless pads of skin to sit on wherever they want. They are also most communicative among monkeys, and even use three different types of yawns to make a point!

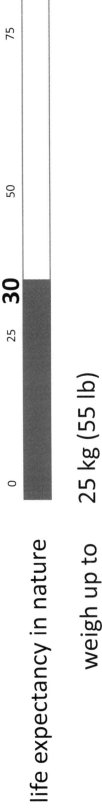

life expectancy in nature

0   25   **30**   50   75   100

weigh up to   25 kg (55 lb)

Jackal

Jackals are similar to wolves and dogs. Although ancient literature in some cultures drew an ugly picture of these animals, they are amazing parents, for instance. They become a pair, they stay faithful to their mate till the end of life and bring up their cubs. They hide the babies in caves or underground dens. And, they change the hiding place every two weeks, so their enemies have very little chance to spot the cubs! What prudency!

life expectancy in nature

0   **14**   25   50   75   100

weigh up to   10 kg (22 lb)

Giraffe

Do you know people who love to bungee jump? Well, they probably got that from a giraffe! A baby giraffe experiences a 1.5-2 meter fall right at his birth, since his mom prefers to give birth standing! Would be fun to need water only once in a few days, too, just like them!

life expectancy in nature

| 0 | 25 | **30** | 50 | 75 | 100 |

weigh up to   1400 kg (3080 lb)

Lemur

Well, folks, enjoy lemurs while you can. The reason? They are the MOST endangered species on the planet. You can find them only on Madagascar and the nearby Comoro Islands. Can you imagine lemurs as big as gorillas? Well, such lemurs are extinct now. Can you see their gorgeous tails? Some lemurs store their fat in their tails to get by during the dry seasons when food is scarce.

life expectancy in nature

20

0   25   50   75   100

weigh up to   3.5 kg (7.7 lb)

Duiker

Duiker got its name from the Afrikaans word which refers to their habit of ducking into bushes when danger is near, while another source describes such movements as zig-zag running style. Guess, they do both when they need to escape predators! They are the most common type of antelopes in Africa.

life expectancy in nature

7

| 0 | 25 | 50 | 75 | 100 |

weigh up to   25 kg (55 lb)

Leopard

If you could choose a perfect spy among the animals, you would vote for leopards. First of all, if all felids could be made one size and their skills compared the leopard would be the strongest! Secondly, they are the most secretive and hard to trace and seen in the wild. Add to the list their ability to run fast, leap up and forward several meters and swim like a fish! Wow, what an incredible set of skills in one body!

life expectancy in nature

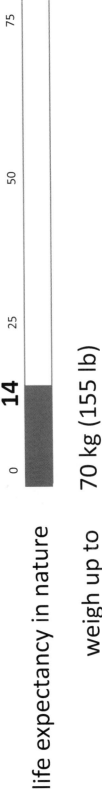

0   **14**   25   50   75   100

weigh up to   70 kg (155 lb)

Okapi

Okapi is a graceful animal which bears the stripes of a zebra and many other features of a giraffe. It has big soft ears that can rotate independently, so the animal can listen for sounds both in front and behind.

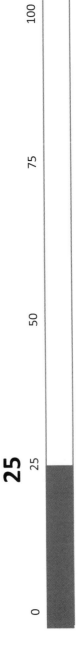

life expectancy in nature

25

weigh up to   250 kg (550 lb)

0   25   50   75   100

Dear Reader!

Thank you for choosing my book! Hope you enjoyed it!

If you really liked it, please, **leave a short review on Amazon!**
Use ISBN # 9781079227536 to find this book

Check out my website http://21centurywritersclub.com/ for more
books by me and my fellow writers!

See ya,
Mark

SEARCH MORE COLORING BOOKS

Book Series: Animal Planet

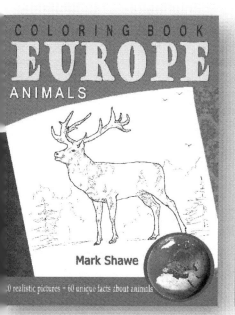

Animals of Europe

ISBN # 9781079222258

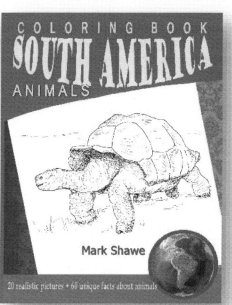

Animals of South America

ISBN # 9781079222920

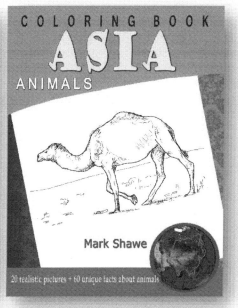

Animals of Asia

ISBN # 9781079224740

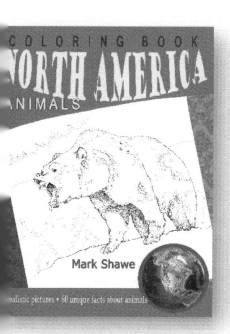

Animals of North America

ISBN # 9781079225525

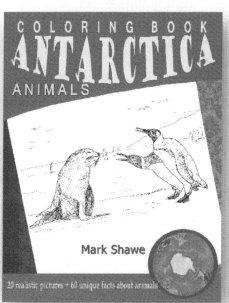

Animals of Antarctica

ISBN # 9781079225969

Animals of Australia

ISBN # 9781079226393

SPECIAL EDITION

COLORING BOOK:
ANIMALS OF THE WORLD

140 original realistic full-page images of wild animals of the World on single-sided sheets to prevent bleed-through

420 interesting unusual facts about the animals

ISBN # 9781079226799

Book Series: **Animal Planet**

Made in United States
Troutdale, OR
10/19/2024

23920031R00027